产品的生产过程

How We Organize Ourselves | Non-Fiction Series

Copyright © 2022 by Level Learning, INC. and Washington Yu Ying PCS™
Original and Edited Text Copyright © 2022 by Washington Yu Ying PCS™

All rights reserved. No part of this book in whole or part may be reproduced without written permission from the publisher.

Published by Level Learning, INC.
Content Contributors:
Washington Yu Ying PCS™ - Feng Dong, Pearl Zao He You
Level Learning - Jingyao Qi

Illustrations by: Josh Taira

Leveling classification based on Level Learning standard.
For full description, visit www.levellearning.com

ISBN 978-1-64040-114-3
Simplified Chinese Edition

About Level Learning:
Level Learning provides a literacy focused curriculum specifically designed for K-12 Chinese as a Second Language classrooms. Our program offers 20 levels of specific and detailed objectives, leveled texts and passages, mastery-based online assessment, and analytics to enable data-driven instruction. Level Learning reading curriculum for both literature and informational text emphasize grammar and comprehension skills to help teachers develop confident and independent Chinese language readers. The non-fiction series of books are specifically designed to support our informational text course based on multiple national standards. To learn more about our entire offering, visit www.levellearning.com.

About Washington Yu Ying PCS™:
Washington Yu Ying PCS is a Mandarin English dual language immersion International Baccalaureate (IB) World school. Yu Ying's mission is to inspire and prepare young people to create a better world by challenging them to reach their full potential in a nurturing Chinese/English educational environment. Yu Ying's comprehensive IB, dual immersion curriculum equips students with global competencies for success in the real world. As a leader in immersion education, Yu Ying is determined to advance Chinese language programs and global citizenry education by helping other schools create and strengthen their Chinese programs. For more information, email: products@washingtonyuying.org

铅笔可以用来写字,汽车可以带你去很多地方。铅笔是一种产品,汽车也是一种产品。

每天我们会看到各种各样的产品，你知道这些产品是怎么生产出来的吗？

首先，生产产品需要材料。生产不一样的产品需要的材料也不一样。比如，做蛋糕需要牛奶，做桌椅需要木头。

接着，人们把材料运到工厂。工人们把这些材料加工成产品。有的产品需要的时间长，有的产品需要的时间短。

然后，工人们会给每一个产品设计一件漂亮的衣服，这件衣服的名字叫做"包装"。

最后，司机们把包装好的产品运到商店、超市、学校、饭店、医院等地方。这样，人们就可以买到他们需要的产品。

人们的需求不一样,所以使用的产品也不一样。

Glossary

	Pinyin	English Definition
铅笔	qiān bǐ	pencil
带	dài	to bring
种	zhǒng	measure word
产品	chǎn pǐn	product
生产	shēng chǎn	to produce
首先	shǒu xiān	first
需要	xū yào	need
材料	cái liào	material
做	zuò	to make
桌椅	zhuō yǐ	table and chair
接着	jiē zhe	next
把	bǎ	to take
运	yùn	to send / to transport
工厂	gōng chǎng	factory
加工	jiā gōng	to process

	Pinyin	English Definition
然后	rán hòu	then
设计	shè jì	to design
包装	bāo zhuāng	package
最后	zuì hòu	last
商店	shāng diàn	store
超市	chāo shì	supermarket
饭店	fàn diàn	restaurant
医院	yī yuàn	hospital
使用	shǐ yòng	to use

www.ingramcontent.com/pod-product-compliance
Lightning Source LLC
Chambersburg PA
CBHW041225070526
44584CB00001B/103